PERSONALIZED PROMISES FOR MOTHERS

DISTINCTIVE SCRIPTURES
PERSONALIZED AND WRITTEN
AS A DECLARATION OF FAITH
FOR YOUR LIFE

by

James R. Riddle

Harrison House
Tulsa, OK

12 11 10 09 08   10 9 8 7 6 5 4 3 2 1

Personalized Promises for Mothers:
Distinctive Scriptures Personalized and Written
as a Declaration of Faith for Your Life
ISBN 13: 978-1-57794-875-9
ISBN 10: 1-57794-875-0
Copyright © 2008 by James R. Riddle
P.O. Box 972624
El Paso, Texas 79997
www.jamesriddle.net

Published by Harrison House, Inc.
P.O. Box 35035
Tulsa, Oklahoma 74153

CONTENTS

INTRODUCTION

One of the wonders of God's Word is how much depth can be found in a single Scripture. One verse can speak volumes of information to us. Consider Hebrews 4:16. This verse alone contains promises of grace, mercy, forgiveness, boldness, closeness with God, answered prayer, spiritual power, and more. I've probably read it a thousand times, and yet each time I read it I am overwhelmed by the fullness of it.

It is my sincere prayer that your life will be changed as you declare each of these promises. Please, daughter of God, don't be duped into thinking that your hardships are God's will. He wants you to live a life full of joy, freedom, and peace. Read His promises. *They* are His will for you. Second Corinthians 1:20 decrees that every one of them is yours. Claim them today and enter into the abundant life that Jesus paid for you to enjoy!

YOU ARE HIS DAUGHTER AND A MEMBER OF DIVINE ROYALTY

Being a man, I can approach this work from a unique perspective. I have a sense of how a father responds to the daughter he loves. Every step she takes, every smile that graces her face, and every new accomplishment in her life is precious in his sight. You, my sister, are God's precious daughter. Even now Daddy is holding you close to His heart. He is with you every moment. He declares your name with pride and sings songs of you in the presence of the angels.

You have no idea how much God's love is pouring through me towards you at this very moment. He loves you dearly. As you read these words, He is looking upon you with such pride it defies description. All of those things you think He is ashamed of are nonexistent in His eyes. He nailed them all to the cross of Jesus, and all He can see now is the perfection of the daughter He loves.

These are the promises that have made you a member of the royal family of God. Meditate on them and speak them in the spirit of faith. Know with certainty that you are a daughter of the King!

1 CHRONICLES 28:6 AMP

He said to me, Solomon your son shall build My house and My courts, for I have chosen him to be My son, and I will be his father.

— DECLARATION OF FAITH —

God is my Father. He chose me to be His own child. I will not forget this great honor.

(Romans 8:29; John 6:37-39; 2 Thessalonians 2:13; Ephesians 1:4,5)

PSALM 68:5,6 NKJV

A father of the fatherless, a defender of widows, is God in His holy habitation.

God sets the solitary in families; He brings out those who are bound into prosperity; but the rebellious dwell in a dry land.

---------- *DECLARATION OF FAITH* ----------

My God is a Father to the fatherless, a defender of the widow, and a companion to the lonely. He leads forth prisoners from their bondage with singing, and as His daughter, I do the same.

(Job 29:11-17; Psalm 10:14; 146:9; James 1:27; Acts 12:6-8; 16:22-26)

PSALM 82:1,6 NKJV

God stands in the congregation of the mighty; He judges among the gods.

I said, "You are gods, and all of you are children of the Most High."

---------- *DECLARATION OF FAITH* ----------

I am created to be like a god in this earth — a very member of the great assembly. I am indeed a daughter of the Most High!

(Genesis 1:26-28; 2 Chronicles 19:6; Psalm 8:4-6; John 10:34; Romans 8:14-17; Ephesians 2:6-10)

MICAH 4:2 NIV

Many nations will come and say, "Come, let us go up to the mountain of the Lord, to the house of the God of Jacob. He will teach us his ways, so that we may walk in his paths." The law will go out from Zion, the word of the Lord from Jerusalem.

——— *DECLARATION OF FAITH* ———

I am God's own daughter—a member of good standing in the royal family.

He continually teaches me His ways so that I may live the God-kind of life.

My days are as the days of heaven, even while I'm on the earth. His Word goes out from me as a seed, in all of its power and authority, and I reap its harvest of goodness every day of my life.

(Mark 4:3-32; Matthew 13:31,32; 17:20; Isaiah 55:11; Romans 8:14; Galatians 4:5)

JOHN 1:12,13 NKJV

As many as received Him, to them He gave the right to become children of God, to those who believe in His name: who were born, not of blood, nor of the will of the flesh, nor of the will of man, but of God.

DECLARATION OF FAITH

I have received Jesus as my own Lord and personal Savior. I have put my complete trust and confidence in His name. I have welcomed Him into my heart and have given Him free reign over my life.

He, in turn, has given me the right and the privilege to become an actual daughter of God. I have been born of God through spiritual regeneration. I was born as out of the womb of the Spirit through the living Word. I am a genuine daughter of almighty God!

(1 Peter 1:4,23; John 3:3-8; Romans 8:29; 10:8-10; Galatians 4:5,6; Titus 3:4-7; 1 John 5:1-5)

TO MAKE YOU A GOOD PARENT

As Dr. Dobson (popular author and founder of Focus on the Family) says, "Parenting isn't for cowards!" We have to be willing to make the tough decisions and display tough love when necessary. We need to set the boundaries for our children and stick to our guns no matter how much it hurts. Discipline is utterly essential if we want our children to live good and wholesome lives. However, discipline is a secondary thing in the role of a good parent.

The Word says to train our children in the nurture and admonition of the Lord. (Eph. 6:4.) Notice that nurture comes first. If we show our children love, spend time with them, become involved in what they are doing, and teach them with a heart of compassion, we will eliminate most of the need to discipline them.

Pray these prayers with the thought of love foremost in your mind. Never forget how your heavenly Father treats you and determine in your heart that you are going to treat your own children in the same way.

DEUTERONOMY 4:9 NKJV

"Only take heed to yourself, and diligently keep yourself, lest you forget the things your eyes have seen, and lest they depart from your heart all the days of your life. And teach them to your children and your grandchildren."

———— *DECLARATION OF FAITH* ————

I attend and give my complete attention to all that the Lord has done for me. I do not let it slip from my mind. I keep these things in the midst of my heart all the days of my life. I will teach them to my children and my grandchildren as long as I have breath within me.

(Deuteronomy 6:4-12; 8:19; 29:2-8; Genesis 18:9; Psalm 103:18; 119:11)

DEUTERONOMY 6:5-13 KJV

Thou shalt love the Lord thy God with all thine heart, and with all thy soul, and with all thy might. And these words, which I command thee this day, shall be in thine heart: And thou shalt teach them diligently unto thy children, and shalt talk of them when thou sittest in thine house, and when thou walkest by the way, and when thou liest down, and when thou risest up. And thou shalt bind them for a sign upon thine hand, and they shall be as frontlets between thine eyes. And thou shalt write them upon the posts of thy house, and on thy gates. And it shall be, when the Lord thy God shall have brought thee into the land which he sware unto thy fathers, to Abraham, to Isaac, and to Jacob, to give thee great and goodly cities, which thou buildedst not, and houses full of all good *things,* which thou filledst not, and wells digged, which thou diggedst not, vineyards and olive trees, which thou plantedst not; when thou shalt have eaten and be full; *then* beware lest thou forget the Lord, which brought thee forth out of the land of Egypt, from the house of bondage. Thou shalt fear the Lord thy God, and serve him, and shalt swear by his name.

DECLARATION OF FAITH

I love my heavenly Father with all of my mind, all of my spirit, and all of my physical strength.

His Word is implanted and deeply rooted in my mind and in my heart.

I whet and sharpen the Word within me that it may pierce through to my mind and my spirit.

I impress the statutes of my God diligently upon the minds of my children. I talk of them when I sit in my house, when I walk by the wayside, when I lie down, and when I rise up. I bind them as a sign on my hand and as an ornament before my eyes. I write them on the door posts of my house and upon my gates.

By these statutes I receive an abundance of blessings.

By the promise of the Lord, I am brought into a prosperous dwelling. Through Him, my home is supplied with an abundance of good things.

All that I have has been given to me by His grace.

It is the Lord who prospers me and gives me an inheritance of things that I did not provide.

I will not forget what He has done for me.

(Deuteronomy 4:29; 8:6-18; Ephesians 3:17; Mark 4:13-20; Psalm 112:1-3; Romans 5:1,2,17; 8:14-17; Philippians 4:19)

JOSHUA 24:15-18 KJV

If it seem evil unto you to serve the Lord, choose you this day whom ye will serve; whether the gods which your fathers served that *were* on the other side of the flood, or the gods of the Amorites, in whose land ye dwell: but as for me and my house, we will serve the Lord. And the people answered and said, God forbid that we should forsake the Lord, to serve other gods; For the Lord our God, he *it is* that brought us up and our fathers out of the land of Egypt, from the house of bondage, and which did those great signs in our sight, and preserved us in all the way wherein we went, and among all the people through whom we passed: And the Lord drave out from before us all the people, even the Amorites which dwelt in the land: *therefore* will we also serve the Lord; for he *is* our God.

——— *DECLARATION OF FAITH* ———

As for me and my house, we will serve the Lord.

Far be it from me to forsake my Father who paid such an awesome price to recreate me in this way.

He brought me out of the land of slavery and from the house of bondage.

He has done great signs and wonders on my behalf and I will not forget it.

(1 Kings 18:21; Psalm 116:16; Exodus 23:24,25; Acts 4:23-31; Colossians 1:13; Luke 4:18)

PROVERBS 19:18 NIV

Discipline your son, for in that there is hope; do not be a willing party to his death.

——— *DECLARATION OF FAITH* ———

I render my children consistent and godly discipline. By this, I give them hope and ensure them a stable future. I refuse to be a party to their destruction, either by restraining from the rod, or by giving it too harshly and without good reason.

(Proverbs 13:24; 22:6; Ephesians 6:4)

PROVERBS 22:6 NIV

Train a child in the way he should go, and when he is old he will not turn from it.

——— *DECLARATION OF FAITH* ———

I consistently train my children in the ways of righteousness. I hold them to the ways of the Lord, so that when they move out on their own, they will be stout against temptation and have the tools to live a blessed and prosperous life.

(Ephesians 6:4; 2 Timothy 3:15; Deuteronomy 6:5-7)

TO CARE FOR
YOUR CHILDREN

When your children suffer, you suffer with them. You hurt every time they hurt. With every tear they shed, you shed even more. You want all that is best for them, and you do everything you can to see that they get it.

God knows your heart, dear mother. He is the One who placed such a caring spirit within you. The prophet Isaiah compares God's love for us to the love of a mother for her newborn child. (Isa. 49:15.) You can know today that God loves your kids dearly and will care for them relentlessly. Read these promises and be comforted; your heavenly Father has made His promise, and He will not let you down. His hands shall surround your children now and forevermore.

EZRA 8:21-23 KJV

Then I proclaimed a fast there, at the river of Ahava, that we might afflict ourselves before our God, to seek of him a right way for us, and for our little ones, and for all our substance. For I was ashamed to require of the king a band of soldiers and horsemen to help us against the enemy in the way: because we had spoken unto the king, saying, The hand of our God *is* upon all them for good that seek him; but his power and his wrath *is* against all them that forsake him. So we fasted and besought our God for this: and he was intreated of us.

—— *DECLARATION OF FAITH* ——

I look to God alone as my safeguard from trouble. He protects my family and me in all circumstances and in every situation. My children dwell in safety within His powerful arms. He takes special care to guard all of those who are with me and sees to it that the enemy does not plunder us.

The Lord answers my every prayer. His gracious hand is upon me because I look to Him alone as my shield.

(Ezra 7:6; Psalm 5:11,12; 23; 33:18,19; Genesis 15:1; Romans 8:28; Malachi 3:11)

PSALM 128:1-4 NKJV

Blessed is every one who fears the Lord, who walks in His ways. When you eat the labor of your hands, you shall be happy, and it shall be well with you. Your wife shall be like a fruitful vine in the very heart of your house, your children like olive plants all around your table. Behold, thus shall the man be blessed who fears the Lord.

———— *DECLARATION OF FAITH* ————

I walk in the ways of almighty God as a good daughter and disciple. I mimic His ways. In every way possible, I live like God lives.

I eat the fruit of my labor and live my life in happiness, peace, divine favor, and good fortune of every kind.

My husband is fruitful and productive within my house, and my children are anointed and blessed at my table.

My life is a pleasure to live.

(Ephesians 5:1; John 10:10; Ecclesiastes 2:24; 3:22;
Psalm 52:8; 144:12; 127:3-5; Proverbs 31:10-31;
1 Peter 3:10,11)

Isaiah 44:1-5 KJV

Yet now hear, O Jacob my servant; and Israel, whom I have chosen: Thus saith the Lord that made thee, and formed thee from the womb, *which* will help thee; Fear not, O Jacob, my servant; and thou, Jesurun, whom I have chosen. For I will pour water upon him that is thirsty, and floods upon the dry ground: I will pour my spirit upon thy seed, and my blessing upon thine offspring: And they shall spring up *as* among the grass, as willows by the water courses. One shall say, I *am* the Lord's; and another shall call *himself* by the name of Jacob; and another shall subscribe *with* his hand unto the Lord, and surname *himself* by the name of Israel.

DECLARATION OF FAITH

I have been chosen by God to be His own daughter. He actually picked me to be a part of His family. He has recreated me in righteousness and helps me in every area of my life. He proclaims His blessing on all that I have and prospers all that I set my hand to do.

God has given me His Word that He will pour out His Spirit and His blessings on my children. They spring up like grass in a meadow—like poplar trees by flowing streams. Their life force is full of health, energy, and vitality. They never go hungry or parched. Each of them is grafted into God's family, taking the name of the Lord as their very own.

(John 15:16-19; Psalm 103:17; Genesis 12:1-3;
Deuteronomy 28:12; Acts 11:14; Ephesians 3:15)

ISAIAH 54:13-17 KJV

All thy children *shall be* taught of the Lord; and great *shall be* the peace of thy children. In righteousness shalt thou be established: thou shalt be far from oppression; for thou shalt not fear: and from terror; for it shall not come near thee. Behold, they shall surely gather together, *but* not by me: whosoever shall gather together against thee shall fall for thy sake. Behold, I have created the smith that bloweth the coals in the fire, and that bringeth forth an instrument for his work; and I have created the waster to destroy. No weapon that is formed against thee shall prosper; and every tongue *that* shall rise against thee in judgment thou shalt condemn. This *is* the heritage of the servants of the Lord, and their righteousness *is* of me, saith the Lord.

— DECLARATION OF FAITH —

My children are taught by the Lord and He gives them tremendous peace and security.

My household is established in righteousness before Him and tyranny cannot gain a foothold in my life.

I have complete authority over all fear, anxiety, stress, and terror. I will not permit them in my life in any shape or form.

If I come under attack in any way, I know it is not the Lord's doing. All of His actions toward me are for

*good and never evil. It is He who gives me strength to
conquer the enemy. Because of this, no weapon formed
against me can prevail over me and I thwart every accu-
sation that comes against me.*

*This is part of my inheritance as God's daughter,
and my righteousness and justification come from Him.*

(Psalm 89:3,4; Jeremiah 29:11; 2 Timothy 1:7; Romans 5:1,2;
8:31,32,37)

ISAIAH 61:6-10 KJV

Ye shall be named the Priests of the Lord: *men* shall call
you the Ministers of our God: ye shall eat the riches of
the Gentiles, and in their glory shall ye boast yourselves.
For your shame *ye shall have* double; and *for* confusion
they shall rejoice in their portion: therefore in their
land they shall possess the double: everlasting joy shall
be unto them. For I the Lord love judgment, I hate
robbery for burnt offering; and I will direct their work
in truth, and I will make an everlasting covenant with
them. And their seed shall be known among the
Gentiles, and their offspring among the people: all that
see them shall acknowledge them, that they *are* the seed
which the Lord hath blessed. I will greatly rejoice in the
Lord, my soul shall be joyful in my God; for he hath
clothed me with the garments of salvation, he hath

covered me with the robe of righteousness, as a bride-
groom decketh *himself* with ornaments, and as a bride
adorneth *herself* with her jewels.

────── *DECLARATION OF FAITH* ──────

*I am known as a priest of the Lord and a minister of
God's power and grace. Instead of shame, I have received
double honor; instead of confusion and disgrace, I leap
for joy in the presence of my Father, for He has given me
a double portion for my inheritance. In His faithfulness,
He has honored His everlasting covenant with me and
has granted me a tremendous reward.*

*My children are blessed because of the covenant.
They shall enjoy the richness of God's inheritance with
me. All who see me will acknowledge that I am a woman
whom God has blessed.*

*I delight in all of these things. My soul rejoices
within me and my spirit pays homage to my Lord and
Father, for He has clothed me with the garments of salvation and arrayed me in a robe of His righteousness.*

(Revelation 1:6; 2 Corinthians 5:20; Job 42:10-12;
Psalm 103:17; 112; Deuteronomy 28:1-14)

A GOOD MARRIAGE

God's promises for a good marriage are promises of guidance. They are promises that will show you what to do to produce the intended result of marital bliss. They are not magic potions. God does not promise to change your husband and make him the person you think he should be, nor does He promise to make him give you the remote control.

What God does promise is that if you give yourself in service and submission, you will sow the seeds that will create a good marriage. It takes work and selfless sacrifice. Never forget that agape love does not seek its own, but the good of the other. When two people go into a marriage with that attitude, only good can come of it.

Of course, submission doesn't mean staying in an abusive marriage. If your husband is abusing you, get help immediately. Talk to your pastor or other ministry leader, or a friend or relative you trust. Or contact a women's shelter, or find a help line in the yellow pages and call it. The point is, don't stay in your home if you are being abused; get help *now*.

A healthy marriage is a life of service, not selfishness. No one should get married unless they have found someone to whom they are willing to give their life in service.

As you pray these prayers, examine your own heart. Make the decision that you are going to do things God's way and He will reward you openly for it.

PROVERBS 5:18,19 KJV

Let thy fountain be blessed: and rejoice with the wife of thy youth. Let her be as the loving hind and pleasant roe; let her breasts satisfy thee at all times; and be thou ravished always with her love.

—— *DECLARATION OF FAITH* ——

My heavenly Father blesses the fountain of my blood, life, and wisdom.

I find great pleasure in my own spouse. He is at the center of all of my sensual desire and is the crowning joy of my life. There is no need for me to look to another for marital fulfillment. I am held captive by his love.

(Deuteronomy 24:5; Ecclesiastes 9:9; Malachi 2:14; Song of Solomon 2:9)

PROVERBS 31:10-31 KJV

Who can find a virtuous woman? for her price *is* far above rubies. The heart of her husband doth safely trust in her, so that he shall have no need of spoil. She will do him good and not evil all the days of her life. She seeketh wool, and flax, and worketh willingly with her hands. She is like the merchants' ships; she bringeth her food from afar. She riseth also while it is yet night, and giveth meat to her household, and a portion to her maidens. She considereth a field, and buyeth it: with the fruit of her hands she planteth a vineyard. She girdeth her loins with strength, and strengtheneth her arms. She perceiveth that her merchandise *is* good: her candle goeth not out by night. She layeth her hands to the spindle, and her hands hold the distaff. She stretcheth out her hand to the poor; yea, she reacheth forth her hands to the needy. She is not afraid of the snow for her household: for all her household *are* clothed with scarlet. She maketh herself coverings of tapestry; her clothing *is* silk and purple. Her husband is known in the gates, when he sitteth among the elders of the land. She maketh fine linen, and selleth *it;* and delivereth girdles unto the merchant. Strength and honour *are* her clothing; and she shall rejoice in time to come. She openeth her mouth with wisdom; and in her tongue *is* the law of kindness. She looketh well to the ways of her household, and eateth not the bread of idleness. Her children arise up, and call her blessed; her husband *also,* and he praiseth her. Many daughters have done virtuously, but thou excellest them all. Favour *is* deceitful, and beauty *is* vain: *but a* woman *that* feareth the Lord, she shall be praised. Give her of the fruit of her hands; and let her own works praise her in the gates.

—— DECLARATION OF FAITH ——

(The confession of a noblewoman—a manifestation of a true daughter of God.)

I am a wife of noble character who is worth far more than rubies to my husband.

My husband has reason to put his complete confidence in me.

I bring him good things all the days of my life and I shall never treat him badly.

As far as I'm concerned, he shall lack nothing of true value and enduring worth.

I am eager to work with my hands and God blesses what I set my hand to do.

I am like a merchant ship bringing in priceless commodities for my family.

I get up while it is still dark to ensure that my family and my servants are well provided for.

I consider my investments wisely. I invest and reinvest until my earnings become like a fruitful vine in a fertile vineyard.

I set about my work vigorously and my arms are strong to complete every task. All of my trading and the work that I have done are profitable, and my lamp does not go out in fearful and troublesome times.

I am diligent and industrious, ever ready to create what is needed for my own life and that of others.

My arms are filled and opened to the poor. Whatever they need, in spirit, soul, or body, I am ready and able to provide.

I have no fear of the blizzard, for my family is clothed warmly and well provided for.

I provide warm and beautiful coverings for my bed and am clothed with the finest that the world can offer.

My husband is respected on account of me. He takes his seat among the rulers of the land.

I am a buyer and a seller, and I gain a tremendous profit from my endeavors.

I am clothed with dignity and strength.

I laugh at the troublesome days to come.

My mouth is full of wisdom and faithful instruction is on my tongue.

I am a faithful guardian over the affairs of my household and will not allow myself to be lazy.

My husband and children arise and call me blessed.

My husband praises me for the blessings that I bring into his life.

The women of the world may do noble things, but I surpass them all. I am a daughter of the living God and I show myself worthy of respect. I earn a tremendous award for my diligence and my name is one to be honored.

(Ruth 3:11; Proverbs 12:4; 19:14; 20:13; Romans 12:11;
Luke 12:42; Genesis 12:1-3; Deuteronomy 8:6-18; 28:12;
Ephesians 4:28; 5:22-24; Philippians 4:19;
1 Corinthians 2:6-16)

MALACHI 2:15,16 NKJV

Did He not make *them* one,
Having a remnant of the Spirit?
And why one?
He seeks godly offspring.
Therefore take heed to your spirit,
And let none deal treacherously with the wife of his youth.
"For the Lord God of Israel says
That He hates divorce,
For it covers one's garment with violence,"
Says the Lord of hosts.
"Therefore take heed to your spirit,
That you do not deal treacherously."

———— *DECLARATION OF FAITH* ————

I guard myself diligently in my spirit so that I may remain faithful to my spouse. Together, God has made us one flesh and we produce godly offspring. Our sons and daughters walk in holiness before the Lord.

I will not disgrace myself by being violent to my spouse in any way, nor will I use divorce as a solution for non-reconciled differences.

I hold these principles as sacred and guard myself diligently in my spirit so that I will not break faith.

(Genesis 2:24; Ephesians 5:22-6:4; Matthew 19:4-12; 1 Corinthians 7:14)

MATTHEW 19:4-6 KJV

He answered and said unto them, Have ye not read, that he which made *them* at the beginning made them male and female, and said, For this cause shall a man leave father and mother, and shall cleave to his wife: and they twain shall be one flesh? Wherefore they are no more twain, but one flesh. What therefore God hath joined together, let not man put asunder.

———— *DECLARATION OF FAITH* ————

I have become one with my husband. God himself has joined us together and we are no longer two, but one flesh.

We are united firmly and joined inseparably in a marital covenant sealed with the blood of Jesus. The bonding agent that holds us together is the very Holy Spirit himself.

Though I honor my parents, I am no longer tied to them. I always maintain proper priorities. I serve God first, my wife second, and my family third.

(Genesis 1:26,27; 2:24; Ephesians 5:22-33; 1 Corinthians 7:3,33)

EPHESIANS 5:22-24, 33 KJV

Wives, submit yourselves unto your own husbands, as unto the Lord. For the husband is the head of the wife, even as Christ is the head of the church: and he is the saviour of the body. Therefore as the church is subject unto Christ, so *let* the wives *be* to their own husbands in every thing. ...and the wife see that she reverence *her* husband.

— *DECLARATION OF FAITH* —

I submit myself to my husband as unto the Lord. I treat my husband as the head (executive in charge) of my life in the same way that Christ is the head (executive in charge) of the Church. So, as the Church submits to Christ, I will submit to my husband in all things, giving him the respect that he deserves.

(1 Corinthians 7:3,4; 11:3; Romans 12:1; Colossians 3:18-4:1; Titus 2:4,5; Proverbs 19:13; 31:10-12,28)

WISDOM

God is wisdom, and He gives wisdom, knowledge, and understanding to those who reverence Him. (Prov. 2:6.) If you have a deep, reverential sense of trust and accountability to Him, then you are on the springboard of all wisdom. That means you know that God is great and awesome in power and majesty. You know that He is faithful and true and is worthy of all praise and adoration.

That means that you have decided to take Him at His Word no matter what the circumstances look like. It means that you know and accept that His knowledge is vastly superior to yours and He knows what needs to be done much more than you do. You know that His Word makes you wiser than your enemies, and even the teachers and philosophers that the world so admires.

You never say such foolish words as, "I know God promised that, *but...*" You are a child of the God of all wisdom and you trust your heavenly Father regardless of what your eyes see, your ears hear, or what is going on around you. You trust Him and receive His wisdom willingly. You know beyond any shadow of doubt that He is causing you to walk in that wisdom every day of your life.

1 KINGS 3:9-14 KJV

Give therefore thy servant an understanding heart to judge thy people, that I may discern between good and bad: for who is able to judge this thy so great a people? And the speech pleased the Lord, that Solomon had asked this thing. And God said unto him, Because thou hast asked this thing, and hast not asked for thyself long life; neither hast asked riches for thyself, nor hast asked the life of thine enemies; but hast asked for thyself understanding to discern judgment; Behold, I have done according to thy words: lo, I have given thee a wise and an understanding heart; so that there was none like thee before thee, neither after thee shall any arise like unto thee. And I have also given thee that which thou hast not asked, both riches, and honour: so that there shall not be any among the kings like unto thee all thy days. And if thou wilt walk in my ways, to keep my statutes and my commandments, as thy father David did walk, then I will lengthen thy days.

—— DECLARATION OF FAITH ——

As God's child, I have a mind of the deepest understanding.

My spirit is perceptive and I have a hearing heart that is discerning between what is right and what is wrong. I clearly discern between the voice of my Father and the voice of the devil.

I seek my Father's kingdom and He is pleased with my prayer life.

I do not set my eyes upon riches to lust after them.

I seek the kingdom of God and His righteousness.

I am focused on attaining a discerning heart of wisdom.

I have been given supernatural ability to obtain and deal rightly with knowledge.

I do not have to worry about riches and protection. God surrounds me with these. I walk in the ways of my Father and do what is right in His sight. He lengthens my days on this earth and grants me the desires of my heart.

(Daniel 1:17,20; 1 John 5:20; 1 Corinthians 1:30; 2:10-16; Matthew 6:19-33; John 10:2-10; 1 Timothy 6:9)

1 CHRONICLES 22:12,13 KJV

Only the Lord give thee wisdom and understanding, and give thee charge concerning Israel, that thou mayest keep the law of the Lord thy God. Then shalt thou prosper, if thou takest heed to fulfil the statutes and judgments which the Lord charged Moses with concerning Israel: be strong, and of good courage; dread not, nor be dismayed.

—— DECLARATION OF FAITH ——

I am a child of wisdom and understanding. I have been anointed with an abundance of wisdom so that I may be greatly successful in my calling.

Everything that I set my hand to do prospers and is brought to unfailing success.

I refuse to give in to fear and doubt. I am not dismayed. I am strong and of good courage, for the Lord is always with me to shield me and give me the victory.

(1 Corinthians 1:30: 2:6-16; 15:57; Daniel 1:17,20; Deuteronomy 28:12; Genesis 39:2-5; James 1:5-8; Joshua 1:5-9)

2 CHRONICLES 9:22,23 AMP

King Solomon surpassed all the kings of the earth in riches and wisdom. And all the kings of the earth sought the presence of Solomon to hear his wisdom which God had put into his mind.

——— *DECLARATION OF FAITH* ———

As an heir of the kingdom of God, I have the promise of riches and wisdom.

People notice the wisdom that God has placed in my mind and they seek my presence for understanding.

(Philippians 4:19; Daniel 1:17,20; 2:22,23;
1 Corinthians 1:30; 2:12)

PSALM 19:7-11 NKJV

The law of the Lord is perfect, converting the soul;

The testimony of the Lord is sure, making wise the simple;

The statutes of the Lord are right, rejoicing the heart;

The commandment of the Lord is pure, enlightening the eyes;

The fear of the Lord is clean, enduring forever;

The judgments of the Lord are true and righteous altogether.

More to be desired are they than gold, yea, than much fine gold; sweeter also than honey and the honeycomb. Moreover by them Your servant is warned, and in keeping them there is great reward.

——— DECLARATION OF FAITH ———

My wisdom comes from the Word of my Father. The perfection of His ways has revived my soul and given joy to my heart. The radiance of His commands is the light by which I see.

The Word is more precious to me than the purest of gold and sweeter to me than honey from the comb. By it, I am warned of all pending danger; and in keeping the statutes therein, I store up the greatest of rewards.

(Psalm 119:72,98-100,130; 1 Corinthians 2:6-10;
Proverbs 8:10,11,19)

EPHESIANS 1:17-23 KJV

That the God of our Lord Jesus Christ, the Father of glory, may give unto you the spirit of wisdom and revelation in the knowledge of him: The eyes of your understanding being enlightened; that ye may know what is the hope of his calling, and what the riches of the glory of his inheritance in the saints, and what *is* the exceeding greatness of his power to us-ward who believe, according to the working of his mighty power, which he wrought in Christ, when he raised him from the dead, and set *him* at his own right hand in the heavenly *places*, far above all principality, and power, and might, and dominion, and every name that is named, not only in this world, but also in that which is to come: And hath put all *things* under his feet, and gave him to be the head over all *things* to the church, which is his body, the fulness of him that filleth all in all.

——— *DECLARATION OF FAITH* ———

My heavenly Father has given me a spirit of wisdom and revelation, of insight into mysteries and secrets, in the deep and intimate knowledge of Himself. My spirit has been enlightened with a flood of understanding so that I can know and comprehend the hope of my calling and the immense riches of this glorious inheritance that has become my own.

I now have a complete understanding of the exceeding greatness of His power toward me. The power that is now residing and working within me is the very power that God wrought in Christ when He raised Him from the dead and seated Him at His own right hand, far above every principality, every power, every ruler of darkness, all dominion and every name or title that can be given. And this power is not only working in and through me now, but it will continue to work in and through me in the age to come. As God has placed all things under Jesus' feet and appointed Him to be the Head of the body (the Church), I have now, as a part of His body, become the fullness of Jesus in this earth as He fills me in every way. All things are placed under my feet and every power and dominion must obey me as I apply the power of attorney that Jesus has given me to use His name.

(Daniel 2:22,23; 1 Corinthians 1:30; 2:6-16;
Matthew 13:11,15,16; 1 John 2:20,27; 5:20; Romans 8:17;
1 Peter 1:3-5; Colossians 1:9-18,26-29; Philippians 2:5-13;
John 14:13,14; 17:20-26; Ephesians 2:6; Hebrews 2:5-14;
Luke 10:19; Mark 16:15-20)

GUIDANCE

In society today we have more distractions than ever that could cause us to stray from the plan that God has for our lives. This is what makes His promises of guidance so precious to us.

There are many ways in which God promises guidance. He guides through His Word, through the fellowship of the Holy Spirit, through pastors and ministers, and sometimes even through the words of children. God may also guide you through a flow of supernatural favor or even by placing obstacles in your path.

No matter how He chooses to guide you, you can rest assured that if you cling to His promises, you will reach the intended destination He has for you. The path may not make much sense, but His Word says that it will be plain. For His very name's sake, He will make sure that you know when you are headed in the right direction.

1 CHRONICLES 10:13,14 KJV

Saul died for his transgression which he committed against the Lord, *even* against the word of the Lord, which he kept not, and also for asking *counsel* of *one that had* a familiar spirit, to enquire *of it*; and enquired not of the Lord: therefore he slew him, and turned the kingdom unto David the son of Jesse.

─────── *DECLARATION OF FAITH* ───────

I am obedient to the Word of God. I do not consult psychics, mediums, and spiritists for guidance. The dead do not guide me. I am guided by the true and living God! I set this forth as a covenant commitment and I will not forget it.

(Deuteronomy 28:1; Leviticus 19:31; Jeremiah 27:9,10; Romans 8:14; John 16:13)

PSALM 25:3-5 NIV

No one whose hope is in you will ever be put to shame, but they will be put to shame who are treacherous without excuse. Show me your ways, O Lord, teach me your paths; guide me in your truth and teach me, for you are God my Savior, and my hope is in you all day long.

─────── *DECLARATION OF FAITH* ───────

I will never be put to shame for trusting in the Lord. He shows me His ways and teaches me His paths so that I have a full understanding of His will for my life. He

*guides me in His truth and reveals to me all that I need
to know to reign as a king in this life. My hope is in Him
every second, of every minute, of every hour, of every day.*

(Romans 1:16; 5:17; 1 Corinthians 2:6-16; Exodus 33:13;
Psalm 5:8-12; 86:11)

ISAIAH 42:16 NKJV

I will bring the blind by a way they did not know; I will
lead them in paths they have not known. I will make
darkness light before them, and crooked places straight.
These things I will do for them, and not forsake them.

——— DECLARATION OF FAITH ———

*The Holy Spirit is always with me to guide and
direct me on the path of life. He turns the darkness into
light before me and makes the rough places smooth. I
have His Word that He will do this and that He will
never leave me nor forsake me.*

(John 16:13; Psalm 119:105; Isaiah 30:21; Hebrews 13:5,6)

EZEKIEL 1:12 NIV

Each one went straight ahead. Wherever the spirit would
go, they would go, without turning as they went.

— *DECLARATION OF FAITH* —

I am led by the Spirit of God. Wherever He goes, I go. I cannot be diverted from the path that He has set before me.

(Romans 8:14; John 16:13; Deuteronomy 28:14)

JOHN 11:9-11 KJV

Jesus answered, Are there not twelve hours in the day? If any man walk in the day, he stumbleth not, because he seeth the light of this world. But if a man walk in the night, he stumbleth, because there is no light in him. These things said he: and after that he saith unto them, Our friend Lazarus sleepeth; but I go, that I may awake him out of sleep.

— *DECLARATION OF FAITH* —

The Light within me guides me in all of my actions in the kingdom just as natural light illuminates my paths in the natural world.

The same goes for the darkness. As anyone who walks in the darkness in the natural world will stumble, so will I stumble if I walk in darkness within the kingdom.

Furthermore, I do not allow the natural world, with its circumstances and obstacles, to guide my actions. If

God calls me to do something, I will do it regardless of what my eyes see, ears hear, or what threatens me in the natural realm.

(1 John 1:5-7; John 1:4,9; 2 Corinthians 5:7; 6:14-18; Hebrews 11:1)

STRENGTH

You can do all things through Christ which strengthens you. Evangelist Kenneth Copeland hit the nail on the head when he declared that this verse in Philippians 4:13 should read: You can do all things through the Anointed One and His anointing which strengthens you. It is the power of God within you that gives you all the strength and ability you need to do what you are called to do.

Other areas of strength can also be found in God's promises. For instance, the joy of the Lord is strength and power for your soul. The Holy Spirit within you is the strength of your life, and the life that He gives you gives strength to your body. In every area that you are personally weak, He is strong within you.

Know that no matter how strong you are in the natural realm, you are always strong in the Lord and in the power of His might. Let these promises sink into your spirit, and be the power force you were created to be.

1 KINGS 2:2,3 NKJV

"I go the way of all the earth; be strong, therefore, and prove yourself a man. And keep the charge of the Lord your God: to walk in His ways, to keep His statutes, His commandments, His judgments, and His testimonies, as it is written in the Law of Moses, that you may prosper in all that you do and wherever you turn."

—— *DECLARATION OF FAITH* ——

I am girded with the strength of almighty God. I walk in the power of His might and show myself to be His daughter. I walk in all of His ways and keep all of His statutes. His precepts and testimonies are forever on my lips.

I am a child of discernment, sound judgment, and discretion. I am enlightened with supernatural ability to learn. God's ways are opened to me and I am bold, shrewd, and wise in all of the ways of life.

In all that I set my hand to do, I am found to be successful and prosperous.

(Deuteronomy 28:12; 29:9; 31:7; Joshua 1:7,8;
1 Chronicles 22:12,13; Daniel 1:17,20)

PSALM 28:7 NKJV

The Lord is my strength and my shield; my heart trusted in Him, and I am helped; therefore my heart greatly rejoices, and with my song I will praise Him.

———— *DECLARATION OF FAITH* ————

The Lord is my ever-present helper. He is always there for me and brings me to victory no matter what situation or circumstance I find myself in. He is my strength and my shield, and I will trust in Him with a steadfast heart.

I leap for joy at the thought of Him. Joyful songs of thanksgiving spring from my heart in adoration of Him.

(Proverbs 3:5,6; Ephesians 5:19; Psalm 13:5; 18:2; 59:17; 112:7)

JEREMIAH 17:5 NIV

This is what the Lord says: "Cursed is the one who trusts in man, who depends on flesh for his strength and whose heart turns away from the Lord."

———— *DECLARATION OF FAITH* ————

I do not put my trust in the ways of man, nor do I rely on the strength of others to sustain me. My trust is

*in the Lord—my provider. He alone is the strength of
my life.*

(Isaiah 30:1,2; Proverbs 3:5,6; Ephesians 6:10)

2 THESSALONIANS 3:3 NIV

The Lord is faithful, and he will strengthen and protect
you from the evil one.

—————— *DECLARATION OF FAITH* ——————

*The Lord is faithful. He strengthens me with His
awesome power and protects me from the strategies of
the evil one. My heavenly Father takes His stand as a
sentinel in my life. He is ever-alert and well able to
maintain His covenant with me and bring me to victory
in every situation.*

(1 Thessalonians 5:24; Luke 10:17-19; Psalm 91;
1 Corinthians 1:9; John 17:15)

2 TIMOTHY 4:17,18 NKJV

The Lord stood with me and strengthened me, so that
the message might be preached fully through me, and
that all the Gentiles might hear. Also I was delivered out
of the mouth of the lion. And the Lord will deliver me

from every evil work and preserve *me* for His heavenly kingdom. To Him *be* glory forever and ever. Amen!

—— DECLARATION OF FAITH ——

The Lord takes His stand at my side, encouraging and strengthening me, so that through me His message might be fully proclaimed to all who will hear it.

He covers me as with a shield, delivering me from the lion's mouth and rescuing me from every evil attack, until that day when I am taken safely into my home in heaven. To God be the glory forever and ever! Amen.

(Matthew 28:20; Hebrews 13:5,6; Romans 8:31;
2 Corinthians 5:18-20; Genesis 15:1; Psalm 5:11,12; 18:1-19;
121:1-8; John 14:1-3)

TO GIVE YOU VISION AND A PURPOSE

God has a plan for your life. It is your own personal mission, and it is unique from all others. Only you can fulfill it. Your very personality—what you love, what you hate, what you enjoy doing, and what drives you with passion—reveals the person you were created to be.

When you take inventory of who you are, you begin to realize what makes you so valuable in the kingdom. No one else can put their heart and soul into your mission the way that you can. You are the absolute best that God has to fulfill your purpose in life.

Right now analyze where you are in your life. Ask your heavenly Father to open the eyes of your understanding and give you a vision of your purpose and how to fulfill it. Write the vision down. Pray over it. Know with certainty that it is the right direction to take—then run with it.

ESTHER 4:14 NIV

"If you remain silent at this time, relief and deliverance for the Jews will arise from another place, but you and your father's family will perish. And who knows but that you have come to royal position for such a time as this?"

—— *DECLARATION OF FAITH* ——

God chose me for a specific purpose. In His infinite wisdom, He has placed me in His kingdom for such a time as this. I am His ideal choice to carry out what He has called me to do. He has given me a mission to fulfill and I intend to fulfill it. I am the best that He has to fulfill my calling. I will not dishonor Him by forcing Him to find another to do my work for me.

(Romans 8:28; 2 Timothy 1:9; 1Timothy 4:14; Acts 9:15; Ephesians 3:7,8)

PSALM 33:11 NIV

The plans of the Lord stand firm forever, the purposes of his heart through all generations.

DECLARATION OF FAITH

My Father's plans and purposes stand firm. They are settled in heaven for all of eternity. I am confident that every one of His promises will be accomplished in my life.

(2 Corinthians 1:20; Proverbs 19:21; Job 23:13; Psalm 119:89,90)

PROVERBS 29:18 KJV

Where *there is* no vision, the people perish: but he that keepeth the law, happy *is* he.

DECLARATION OF FAITH

I clearly understand what I am called to do in the kingdom. I have a vision—a revelation of His redemption as it applies to my life.

I am obedient to the Word.

I am fixed in the covenant and happy, fortunate and enviable in all of my ways.

(Habakkuk 2:2; 1 Samuel 3:1; Amos 8:11,12; Proverbs 8:32; John 13:17)

LUKE 5:19 NKJV

So also were James and John, the sons of Zebedee, who were partners with Simon. And Jesus said to Simon, "Do not be afraid. From now on you will catch men."

———— *DECLARATION OF FAITH* ————

I have absolutely no fear of my calling in Christ. I am thoroughly equipped with the ability to do what He has called me to do. I am a fisher of men with a distinct role to fulfill in the great design of redemption.

(Joshua 1:5-8; 2 Corinthians 2:14; 6:1; Philippians 1:6; 2:12,13; 4:13; 1 Peter 4:11)

2 PETER 1:10,11 NKJV

Therefore, brethren, be even more diligent to make your call and election sure, for if you do these things you will never stumble; for so an entrance will be supplied to you abundantly into the everlasting kingdom of our Lord and Savior Jesus Christ.

———— *DECLARATION OF FAITH* ————

I make it my business to establish myself firmly in my calling so that I will never fail in the things that I am called to do. In doing so, I have assurance that one day I will receive a rich welcome into the eternal kingdom of my Lord and Savior Jesus Christ.

In every way I will be the person that God created me to be.

(Romans 11:29; 1 John 3:19; Philippians 1:12,13; Luke 16:9)

COURAGE AND BOLDNESS

The Lord has declared that He has not given you a spirit of fear, but of power, love, and a sound mind. (2 Tim. 1:7.) Think about that. The Lord himself dwells within you. He is on your side in every circumstance that you face. What is there to be afraid of? Is He not more powerful than your enemies? Has He not told you to be strong and of good courage for He is with you wherever you go? (Deut. 31:6.) *Any* fear that comes against you is from the enemy. It is designed to rob you of your faith and make you stagnant in your walk with God.

The devil knows that if the daughter of God stands with courage and moves forward in boldness, his strategies will be thwarted and his kingdom will fall. Be a thorn in his side, my sister. Be the fearless daughter of God that you are intended to be.

DEUTERONOMY 1:21 NKJV

"Look, the Lord your God has set the land before you; go up *and possess it*, as the Lord God of your fathers has spoken to you; do not fear or be discouraged."

———— *DECLARATION OF FAITH* ————

The Lord has set the land before me. I am not afraid. I will go forth and possess it, for He has made me well able.

(Joshua 1:5-9; 23:9-11; Romans 8:31; Numbers 14:8;
Philippians 4:13)

JUDGES 6:12-14 KJV

The angel of the Lord appeared unto him, and said unto him, The Lord *is* with thee, thou mighty man of valour. And Gideon said unto him, Oh my Lord, if the Lord be with us, why then is all this befallen us? and where *be* all his miracles which our fathers told us of, saying, Did not the Lord bring us up from Egypt? but now the Lord hath forsaken us, and delivered us into the hands of the Midianites. And the Lord looked upon him, and said, Go in this thy might, and thou shalt save Israel from the hand of the Midianites: have not I sent thee?

——— *DECLARATION OF FAITH* ———

I am a warrior in the army of God. I am intrepid—full of courage and valor—and the Lord is with me in everything that I do.

I do not allow circumstances to direct my faith. I go forward fearlessly in the will and power of almighty God.

It is my Father, the God of the entire universe, that has sent me to do His work. He has ordained me in my calling. He has anointed (empowered) me and I am well able to do what He has called me to do.

(Ephesians 6:10-18; Joshua 1:5-9; Isaiah 41:10;
Philippians 2:12,13; Romans 11:29; 1 John 2:27)

1 CHRONICLES 19:13 AMP

Be of good courage and let us behave ourselves courageously for our people and for the cities of our God; and may the Lord do what is good in His sight.

——— *DECLARATION OF FAITH* ———

I am strong and very courageous! My actions are not birthed in fear, but in courage. I am a bold and fearless child of the living God! I stand up courageously for my people! Through me, the Lord does what is good and right in this earth!

(Joshua 1:5-9; 2 Timothy 1:7; Philippians 2:12,13; 1 John 4:1-4)

MARK 5:36 NKJV

As soon as Jesus heard the word that was spoken, He said to the ruler of the synagogue, "Do not be afraid; only believe."

—— DECLARATION OF FAITH ——

When I am faced with an evil report in the natural realm, I remain calm and continue to believe. I do not allow fear to rob me of what God has done for me. My faith brings to pass what I need regardless of what is seen or known in the natural world.

(Numbers 14:1-9; 2 Timothy 1:6,7; Joshua 1:5-9;
2 Corinthians 5:7; Hebrews 11:1)

PHILIPPIANS 1:19-24 KJV

I know that this shall turn to my salvation through your prayer, and the supply of the Spirit of Jesus Christ, According to my earnest expectation and *my* hope, that in nothing I shall be ashamed, but *that* with all boldness, as always, *so* now also Christ shall be magnified in my body, whether *it be* by life, or by death. For to me to live *is* Christ, and to die *is* gain. But if I live in the flesh, this *is* the fruit of my labour: yet what I shall choose I wot not. For I am in a strait betwixt two, having a desire to depart, and to be with Christ; which is far better: Nevertheless to abide in the flesh *is* more needful for you.

DECLARATION OF FAITH

No matter what is going on in my life or what my situation may be, I know that through the help of the Spirit of Jesus and the prayers of God's people, I shall be delivered and stand as a victor to the praise and the glory of God.

I remain in eager expectation and the assurance of hope. I persevere through every trial and stand my ground regardless of the circumstances. I never cower in shame because of my faith. My walk with Jesus is one of persistent courage and unwavering boldness. I refuse to give up on my faith, for I know that He who promised is faithful. He will do what He said He would do.

(Hebrews 9:27; 10:23,35-11:1; Acts 12:5-10; Isaiah 46:4; 55:11; Romans 8:11; |2 Corinthians 9:5-11; John 14:1-3; 15:5; Deuteronomy 30:19,20; Matthew 28:18-20; Job 13:16; 2 Timothy 4:6; Psalm 16:11; 91:16)

REST AND REJUVENATION

So many people, especially in the ministry, become obsessed with their work. They lose sight of the joys of living, and the result is often failed health, failed marriages, friendships dissolved, etc. God did not intend for you to be so unbalanced in your career. He did not create you to be a workaholic. He wants you to have regular rest so that life isn't overwhelming. God himself rested on the seventh day. Jesus even commanded His disciples to take a break and relax in spite of all the work that had to be done.

There are also promises here of restful sleep. God wants you to feel so secure about your life that nothing brings you anxiety. When you sleep it should be sweet so that when you awake, you are refreshed and ready to meet a new day.

1 KINGS 8:56 KJV

Blessed *be* the Lord, that hath given rest unto his people Israel, according to all that he promised: there hath not failed one word of all his good promise, which he promised by the hand of Moses his servant.

——— *DECLARATION OF FAITH* ———

The Lord has given me rest.

All of His promises to me are manifested in my life. None of His promises fail me. Not one word that my Father has spoken to me fails to come to pass.

(Deuteronomy 12:10; Hebrews 3; 2 Corinthians 1:20; Isaiah 55:11)

JOB 11:19 NKJV

You would also lie down, and no one would make *you* afraid; *Yes,* many would court your favor.

——— *DECLARATION OF FAITH* ———

I remain safe and secure in the hands of my heavenly Father. I go to sleep at night with no one to make me afraid.

Many shall see God's blessings on my life and court my favor.

(Psalm 4:8; 23; Deuteronomy 28:10; Ephesians 1:3;
John 10:28,29; Job 29:7-25)

PSALM 3:5-7 AMP

I lay down and slept; I wakened again, for the Lord sustains me. I will not be afraid of ten thousands of people who have set themselves against me round about. Arise, O Lord; save me, O my God! For You have struck all my enemies on the cheek; You have broken the teeth of the ungodly.

—— *DECLARATION OF FAITH* ——

I stretch myself out to sleep in perfect peace, free of all anxiety.

When my rest is complete, I awake again and find the Lord at my side, keeping guard over my life. He is an ever-present sentinel who never fails to protect me from the attacks of my enemies. I will not fear even tens of thousands drawn up against me, for I am never alone. The Lord of Hosts is my companion and ally. He strikes my enemies down in a fierce display of His power. His mighty fist shatters their teeth.

So let the enemy bark all he wants. His bite is nothing to me.

(Leviticus 26:6; Psalm 4:8; 23:4; 27:3; 121; 127:2; Exodus 23:20-30; 1 John 4:1-4)

MATTHEW 11:27-30 KJV

All things are delivered unto me of my Father: and no man knoweth the Son, but the Father; neither knoweth any man the Father, save the Son, and *he* to whomsoever the Son will reveal *him.* Come unto me, all *ye* that labour and are heavy laden, and I will give you rest. Take my yoke upon you, and learn of me; for I am meek and lowly in heart: and ye shall find rest unto your souls. For my yoke *is* easy, and my burden is light.

——— DECLARATION OF FAITH ———

I am born to fully know and accurately understand the things of God. Jesus, my Lord and my brother, has given me a thorough revelation of our Father's being.

I cast all of the heavy burdens of my life upon Jesus. They are now upon His shoulders and I am set free. All that has weighed me down is now His to bear.

I have taken His yoke upon me and have made Him the center of all of my learning. I find comfort in His gentleness and simplicity. In Him, I have found rest, relief, and refreshment for my soul.

The yoke that I have been given is easy to bear. It is life to me in abundance.

(1 Corinthians 2:6-16; 1 John 5:20; 1 Peter 5:5-7;
John 6:35-37; 10:10)

MARK 6:31 NKJV

He said to them, "Come aside by yourselves to a deserted place and rest a while." For there were many coming and going, and they did not even have time to eat.

— DECLARATION OF FAITH —

I will not allow life to become so hectic for me that I have no leisure time. It is not the will of my Father that I be overwhelmed that way. Therefore, I will regularly take time to rest and enjoy the blessings that He has given me.

(Ecclesiastes 2:24; 3:22; Matthew 11:28-30; 14:13)

FAVOR

Favor is God's supernatural influence, which brings you partiality and preeminence in every situation. It is the one thing that gives you an advantage over every person outside the kingdom of God. God rains His general blessings upon the just and the unjust alike, but His blessing of favor is given exclusively to His children.

Too many of us overlook the favor that God gives us. Never forget that God wants you to have all of the best things in life. Don't allow false humility to rob you of this blessing. If someone wants to do something nice for you, thank them and enjoy the favor. If someone hands you a $100 bill, thank them for it. Be appreciative of the good things done for you. It blesses the giver when you appreciate what they are doing. Don't pray for favor and then reject it when God gives it. Just be thankful and enjoy it.

GENESIS 39:20-23 KJV

Joseph's master took him, and put him into the prison, a place where the king's prisoners were bound: and he was there in the prison. But the Lord was with Joseph, and shewed him mercy, and gave him favour in the sight of the keeper of the prison. And the keeper of the prison committed to Joseph's hand all the prisoners that were in the prison; and whatsoever they did there, he was the doer of it. The keeper of the prison looked not to any thing that was under his hand; because the Lord was with him, and that which he did, the Lord made it to prosper.

——— *DECLARATION OF FAITH* ———

No matter what the circumstances may be in my life, I prosper, for the Lord is with me to show me mercy, loving-kindness, and an abundance of favor with all of those I come in contact with. I have favor with my employers, my pastors, my teachers and my administrators. They see that I am called to be a leader and the Lord makes everything that I am put in charge of to prosper.

(Psalm 1:1-3; 5:11,12; 23; Genesis 12:1-3; 30:29,30; 39:2-5; Deuteronomy 28:1-14)

EZRA 7:27,28 NIV

Praise be to the Lord, the God of our fathers, who has put it into the king's heart to bring honor to the house of the Lord in Jerusalem in this way and who has extended his good favor to me before the king and his advisers and all the king's powerful officials. Because the hand of the Lord my God was on me, I took courage and gathered leading men from Israel to go up with me.

——— *DECLARATION OF FAITH* ———

I take courage to do all that the Lord has commanded. He has given me favor with the rulers of this world and with their officials. He has set me in a position of high honor among them. Therefore, I am bold to take my place in His army and go forward to do His work.

(Joshua 1:5-9; Psalm 5:11,12; 91:15,16; Genesis 39:2-5; Ephesians 2:6)

PROVERBS 8:35 NKJV

Whoever finds me finds life, and obtains favor from the Lord.

——— *DECLARATION OF FAITH* ———

My love for wisdom has brought me energy, spunk, vitality, and God's own favor. I will walk this life fully expecting God's blessings to come my way.

(Proverbs 3:3-6; John 17:3; Isaiah 61:1-3; Ephesians 1:3)

LUKE 1:28 NKJV

Having come in, the angel said to her, "Rejoice, highly favored one, the Lord is with you; blessed are you among women!"

——— *DECLARATION OF FAITH* ———

Like Mary, God has set me apart as one who is unique and special. He makes His declaration to all that I am one of His favored ones and that He is with me in all that I do.

(Isaiah 43:1-7; Hebrews 10:14-17; 13:5,6; Matthew 28:20; Psalm 103:13; Job 1:8)

ACTS 27:3 NKJV

The next *day* we landed at Sidon. And Julius treated Paul kindly and gave *him* liberty to go to his friends and receive care.

——— *DECLARATION OF FAITH* ———

I continually walk in God's favor and people go out of their way to do nice things for me.

(Proverbs 3:3,4; Genesis 12:1-3; Exodus 3:21,22; 11:3; 12:36)

FRIENDS

It is a horrible thing to be alone in the world. When God created Adam, He declared that it was not good for him to be alone. If you read 3 John 1, or John 14 through 17, you cannot help but notice that God wants you to be a part of a circle of friends. We all need each other for support and encouragement. We are all members of one Body, and we cannot do what God wants us to do unless we do it together.

So where do you find your friends? Hebrews 10:24-25 tells us that our friends are found in a local church. Yet that is just the first step. You cannot gain friends by just attending. You must get involved. Go to the various church functions. Become a volunteer.

God wants to bring you into fellowship with other Christians with whom you can connect. Even now He has someone that you have yet to meet. And even more beautiful is the fact that every friend in Christ is a friend for all of eternity.

PROVERBS 13:20 KJV

He that walketh with wise men shall be wise: but a companion of fools shall be destroyed.

—— *DECLARATION OF FAITH* ——

I choose my friends wisely. I am a companion of the wise, not of fools.

I have proven the path of wisdom and my insight is watered for continuous growth.

(2 Corinthians 6:14; Ephesians 5:1-14; 1 Corinthians 5:9)

ECCLESIASTES 4:9-12 KJV

Two are better than one; because they have a good reward for their labour. For if they fall, the one will lift up his fellow: but woe to him *that is* alone when he falleth; for *he hath* not another to help him up. Again, if two lie together, then they have heat: but how can one be warm *alone?* And if one prevail against him, two shall withstand him; and a threefold cord is not quickly broken.

—— *DECLARATION OF FAITH* ——

I am wise to seek godly companionship in the things that I do. I understand that two can bring in a better harvest than one, for if one of us falls, the other can lift him (or her) up. Furthermore, if one of us is overpowered, the other can step in and lend a hand so that we can withstand every foe.

I am not an island in my walk with God. I am a companion of God's children and together, with God entwined in us and through us, we will be victorious in every situation.

(Proverbs 15:22; Ephesians 5:1-18; Hebrews 10:25; Deuteronomy 32:30)

LUKE 17:3,4 KJV

Take heed to yourselves: If thy brother trespass against thee, rebuke him; and if he repent, forgive him. And if he trespass against thee seven times in a day, and seven times in a day turn again to thee, saying, I repent; thou shalt forgive him.

— DECLARATION OF FAITH —

I am ever-alert and prepared to act on the behalf of my brothers and sisters in Christ. I look out for them just as I look out for myself.

I will not allow bitterness and strife to come between us and hinder our prayers or stop the flow of blessings provided in our covenant with God and each other. No matter how many times a brother or sister sins against *me, I forgive them. Resentment finds no home in my heart and all offenses against me I consider to be annulled, eradicated, and expunged from our relationship.*

(Psalm 106:29-31; Mark 11:25; Matthew 6:12; 18:15-21; Proverbs 17:10)

ROMANS 1:11,12 KJV

I long to see you, that I may impart unto you some spiritual gift, to the end ye may be established; that is, that I may be comforted together with you by the mutual faith both of you and me.

—— *DECLARATION OF FAITH* ——

I yearn for those times when I can gather together with my brothers and sisters in Christ so I can share my spiritual gifts with them to strengthen and encourage them in their faith.

I know the power of the corporate anointing and consciously seek the gifts of others in order to strengthen my faith as well.

(Hebrews 10:25; 1 Corinthians 12:1,7; 14:3; 2 Timothy 1:6; 2 Peter 1:3; 3:1)

Ephesians 4:1-3 NIV

As a prisoner for the Lord, then, I urge you to live a life worthy of the calling you have received. Be completely humble and gentle; be patient, bearing with one another in love. Make every effort to keep the unity of the Spirit through the bond of peace.

—————— *DECLARATION OF FAITH* ——————

I stir myself up to live a life worthy of the calling that I have received. I am completely humble, unselfish, gentle, and patient, bearing with my brothers and sisters in Christ, making allowances (being merciful, lenient, and compassionate) because of my love for them. I make every effort to maintain a unity in the body of Christ, in the Spirit, through the binding power of peace.

(Hebrews 10:24; 1 Thessalonians 2:12; James 4:1-10; Galatians 6:1,2; Romans 16:17-20; Colossians 3:14)

COMFORT AND ENCOURAGEMENT

These promises hold a special place in my heart. On the morning of June 23, 1999, I received news that my precious wife had been killed in a horrible traffic accident. Up to that moment in my life I had never really known grief. All of my plans and my vision for life were crushed in a moment of time. My body felt as if it were giving out because of the depth of my pain.

I remember thinking that I had to get to church; I had to be with my church family; I had to be lifted in prayer or I would surely grieve myself to death. I remember how my pastor, Rochelle, embraced me like a mother and shed her tears with mine. I remember literally feeling the prayers of the church lifting me up. But more than anything else, I remember God's comfort. His son was hurting and He hated every minute of it. I could almost feel Him lifting me to His chest and holding me with every wave of grief.

I can tell you of a certainty that our Father truly is the God of all comfort. No matter what you are facing,

He will comfort and strengthen you so that you can rise again and fulfill the call He has on your life. He is always there for you, my sister. Never forget that.

RUTH 2:12 NIV

"May the Lord repay you for what you have done. May you be richly rewarded by the Lord, the God of Israel, under whose wings you have come to take refuge."

—— DECLARATION OF FAITH ——

I have taken refuge under my Father's wing and He has given me a full reward. Though I was not a part of His family, He has adopted me, recreated me so that I am actually born again as His own daughter, and has given me all of the rights and privileges of an heir to His kingdom. He has comforted me and given me abundant favor in His sight.

(1 Samuel 24:19; Psalm 17:8; 36:7; 58:11; 91:1-4; Galatians 4:4-6; Romans 8:14-17; 2 Corinthians 1:3,4; 5:17)

PSALM 34:18-22 NKJV

The Lord is near to those who have a broken heart, and saves such as have a contrite spirit. Many are the afflictions of the righteous, but the Lord delivers him out of them all. He guards all his bones; not one of them is broken. Evil shall slay the wicked, and those who hate the righteous shall be condemned. The Lord redeems the soul of His servants, and none of those who trust in Him shall be condemned.

—— DECLARATION OF FAITH ——

My Father comforts me when I am brokenhearted. When my spirit is crushed and I feel alone, He wraps His tender arms around me and embraces me in His love.

I am faced with troubles of many kinds, but the Lord delivers me out of every one.

I am identified with Jesus in every way. All that He did is set to my account. Therefore, I can count on my Father to protect me from all danger so that none of my bones can be broken.

Evil shall slay those who come against me and those who hate the righteousness I have chosen shall be desolate.

Through it all I stand unscathed. I am a redeemed and reborn daughter of the living God! There is absolutely no condemnation for me, for I have taken my refuge in the Lord.

(Acts 17:28; Psalm 51:17; 145:18; Proverbs 24:16; Genesis 12:1-3; 2 Timothy 3:12; Romans 8:1)

PSALM 71:20,21 NIV

Though you have made me see troubles, many and bitter, you will restore my life again; from the depths of the earth you will again bring me up. You will increase my honor and comfort me once again.

—— *DECLARATION OF FAITH* ——

When troubles overwhelm me and it seems the weight of the world is on my shoulders, God shall quicken me once again. Though many distresses and misfortunes have rained upon me, I shall rise with the strength and power of heaven in my wake. God takes His stand with me in every circumstance. He increases my greatness and comforts me on every side.

(Psalm 34:6-8; Proverbs 24:16; Ephesians 6:10; Genesis 12:1-3; Exodus 14:13,14)

JOHN 16:7-11 KJV

Nevertheless I tell you the truth; It is expedient for you that I go away: for if I go not away, the Comforter will not come unto you; but if I depart, I will send him unto you. And when he is come, he will reprove the world of sin, and of righteousness, and of judgment: Of sin, because they believe not on me; of righteousness, because I go to my Father, and ye see me no more; of judgment, because the prince of this world is judged.

─── *DECLARATION OF FAITH* ───

It is to my advantage that Jesus has gone on to heaven to take His place at the right hand of the Father. Because He has gone, the Holy Spirit, my Comforter, Counselor, and strength, has come to me.

He is ever with me in close fellowship, revealing to me all that I need to know.

It is He who has revealed to me my deliverance from sin and right standing in the eyes of God.

He gives me a direct revelation of Satan's defeat and a full understanding of my rights, privileges, and authority in Jesus.

(Acts 1:5,8; 2:33; John 16:13; Ephesians 1:13-23;
1 Corinthians 2:6-16; Luke 10:18,19)

2 CORINTHIANS 1:3-5 KJV

Blessed be God, even the Father of our Lord Jesus Christ, the Father of mercies, and the God of all comfort; Who comforteth us in all our tribulation, that we may be able to comfort them which are in any trouble, by the comfort wherewith we ourselves are comforted of God. For as the suffering of Christ abound in us, so our consolation also aboundeth by Christ.

——— *DECLARATION OF FAITH* ———

My heavenly Father is the Father of mercies and the God of all comfort. His compassion toward me is boundless. He comforts, encourages, and assists me through all of life's troubles, so that I can comfort, encourage, and assist others who are going through the same things that I have gone through.

I am also identified with Christ's sufferings. Therefore, through my oneness with Him, I have every ability to comfort others no matter what they are going through. For in the same way I am identified with Christ's sufferings, so also does His comfort, encouragement, and assistance flow through me in abundance.

(John 14:16,17; Isaiah 51:12; 66:13; Galatians 2:20; Colossians 1 27-29)

TO NEVER FAIL YOU

This ties into the category of God honoring His Word but is worthy to stand on its own. The reason I say this is because it is possible to be emotionally damaged by people who have made us promises that they never intended to keep. This is especially heartbreaking when those people who have failed us are our own parents.

God is your Father, and He doesn't want to be compared to an earthly father who doesn't really care about his child. God is good to you. He will never lie to you. You can trust Him unwaveringly, for He will never let you down.

Read these promises and take heart. God will make good on every one.

1 SAMUEL 30:6 NKJV

David was greatly distressed, for the people spoke of stoning him, because the soul of all the people was grieved, every man for his sons and his daughters. But David strengthened himself in the Lord his God.

──────── *DECLARATION OF FAITH* ────────

When turmoil comes in like a flood, I will encourage myself in the Lord. I look to God and His Word for my confidence.

When others fail me and forsake me, God takes His stand on my behalf. Together, we overcome any and every problem that I may face.

(Isaiah 25:4; 59:19; Habakkuk 3:17-19; 2 Timothy 1:6; Acts 4:23-31)

1 CHRONICLES 28:19,20 NIV

"All this," David said, "I have in writing from the hand of the Lord upon me, and he gave me understanding in all the details of the plan." David also said to Solomon his son, "Be strong and courageous, and do the work. Do not be afraid or discouraged, for the Lord God, my God, is with you. He will not fail you or forsake you until all the work for the service of the temple of the Lord is finished."

──────── *DECLARATION OF FAITH* ────────

My Father gives me understanding in all that He has called me to do. I am well able to accomplish every task that is set before me. I have no reason to fear or be dismayed. I am strong and very courageous. I will not forget that my Father God is with me in everything that I do. He will not fail me. He sees to it that I have all that I need and stays with me as an ever-present help until all of the work is finished.

(1 Corinthians 2:6-16; 1 John 5:20; Daniel 1:17,20;
Joshua 1:5-9; Hebrews 13:5,6)

NEHEMIAH 9:16-21 KJV

But they and our fathers,…refused to obey, neither were mindful of thy wonders that thou didst among them; but hardened their necks, and in their rebellion appointed a captain to return to their bondage: but thou *art* a God ready to pardon, gracious and merciful, slow to anger, and of great kindness, and forsookest them not. Yea, when they had made them a molten calf, and said, This is thy God that brought thee up out of Egypt, and had wrought great provocations; Yet thou in thy manifold mercies forsookest them not in the wilderness: the pillar of the cloud departed not from them by day, to lead them in the way; neither the pillar of fire by night, to shew them light, and the way wherein they should go. Thou gavest also thy good spirit to instruct them, and withheldest not thy manna from their mouth, and gavest them water for their thirst. Yea, forty years didst thou sustain them in the wilderness, *so that* they lacked nothing; their clothes waxed not old, and their feet swelled not.

DECLARATION OF FAITH

My heavenly Father is forgiving and compassionate toward me. He grants me His unmerited favor as a free gift. His patience and love towards me have no end. He has given me His Word that He will never leave me nor forsake me.

Even when my faith has failed, He has remained faithful to me. He has never withheld His manna from my mouth and has always given me water for my thirst.

He has given me the Holy Spirit to instruct me in all of my ways.

He sustains me in every situation so that I lack no good thing. My clothes are not worn and ragged and my feet never swell from my journey in the life that He has called me to live.

(Psalm 103:1-18; Hebrews 13:5,6; John 16:13; Psalm 34:10; 106:45; Joel 2:13)

JOB 31:24-28 KJV

If I have made gold my hope, or have said to the fine gold, *Thou art* my confidence; if I rejoiced because my wealth *was* great, and because mine hand had gotten much; if I beheld the sun when it shined, or the moon walking *in* brightness; and my heart hath been secretly enticed, or my mouth hath kissed my hand: This also *were* an iniquity *to be punished by* the judge: for I should have denied the God *that is* above.

———— DECLARATION OF FAITH ————

I do not put my trust in gold as my security, nor do I rejoice over the great riches that I have been given, or the fortune that I have gained by what I have set my hand to do. My heart cannot be secretly enticed to pay homage to any provider but one: The Lord my God! My faith and trust are in Him and Him alone!

(Matthew 6:19-33; 1 Timothy 6:17; Mark 10:17-25; Psalm 62:10; Deuteronomy 8:18)

LAMENTATIONS 3:22-26 KJV

It is of the Lord's mercies that we are not consumed, because his compassions fail not. *They are* new every morning: great *is* thy faithfulness. The Lord *is* my portion, saith my soul; therefore will I hope in him. The Lord *is* good unto them that wait for him, to the soul *that* seeketh him. *It is* good that *a man* should both hope and quietly wait for the salvation of the Lord.

———— *DECLARATION OF FAITH* ————

God's compassion for me never fails. He renews His love and blessings for me every morning and is faithful to fulfill the plan He has for my life.

I am His highest priority and He makes it His business to bless me.

He carefully watches over me so that I am not overrun by the enemy.

The Lord is my portion and my delight. I will wait for Him in the midst of adversity. I wait quietly for His salvation. He is always faithful and comes through for me every time.

God is not only good to me some of the time, He is good to me all of the time. He has given me His Word that He will never harm me in any way.

(Romans 8:38,39; Jeremiah 29:11; Isaiah 30:15; 40:28-31; Deuteronomy 6:24; Psalm 16:5; 78:38; 119:57,65)

PROTECTION

When I wrote the introduction in the love chapter on God giving us the ability to love others, this chapter on protection was in the back of my mind the whole time. Even though we are to love our enemies, sometimes we need to protect ourselves from them. That means that there are times even when we should pray that they are taken out of our way. That goes for enemies in this natural world as well as our spiritual enemies.

One name that comes to mind as a natural world enemy is Osama bin Laden. I hold fast to some of the following promises against him. I believe that he will be found out and utterly brought to justice. The Word teaches us that there are times when extreme measures are to be taken for the greater good. If an enemy threatens the life of your family, you protect your family first. They are what is most important.

This concept comes straight from the heart of your Father. If someone threatens His children, He takes it personally. He will protect you with a vengeance. The following promises are testimony to that fact.

Exodus 12:23 AMP

The Lord will pass through to slay the Egyptians; and when He sees the blood upon the lintel and the two side posts, the Lord will pass over the door and will not allow the destroyer to come into your houses to slay you.

——— *DECLARATION OF FAITH* ———

When the destroyer comes to put plagues on the world, the Lord will not allow him to come into my house.

A hedge and a shield of protection have been built around my family and the destroyer cannot touch us.

The blood of the Lamb is upon my household. Therefore, I remain safe.

(1 John 5:18; Job 1:10; 1 Corinthians 5:7; Isaiah 53:4-7; Psalm 91:10)

Proverbs 1:33 NKJV

"Whoever listens to me will dwell safely, and will be secure, without fear of evil."

——— *DECLARATION OF FAITH* ———

I heed the ways of wisdom and live my life in safety. I am at peace—free from the fear that comes from an evil report.

(Numbers 14:8; Proverbs 3:24-26; Psalm 112:7)

Ezekiel 34:11,12 NIV

"This is what the Sovereign Lord says: I myself will search for my sheep and look after them. As a shepherd looks after his scattered flock when he is with them, so will I look after my sheep. I will rescue them from all the places where they were scattered on a day of clouds and darkness."

——— *DECLARATION OF FAITH* ———

My Father's protective eye never leaves me. He looks after me as a good shepherd looks after his flock when he is with them.

(Nehemiah 1:5,6; Job 36:7; Psalm 3:5,6; 11:4; John 10:11-18)

Joel 3:16 NKJV

The Lord also will roar from Zion, and utter His voice from Jerusalem; the heavens and earth will shake; but the Lord will be a shelter for His people, and the strength of the children of Israel.

——— *DECLARATION OF FAITH* ———

No matter what the circumstances may hold, or what is coming against those around me, I stand safe and secure. My refuge is the Creator of the heavens and the earth. He is my Lord and my Father—my stronghold in times of trouble.

(Psalm 91; Isaiah 51:5,6; Proverbs 12:21)

ACTS 28:3-5 KJV

When Paul had gathered a bundle of sticks, and laid them on the fire, there came a viper out of the heat, and fastened on his hand. And when the barbarians saw the *venomous* beast hang on his hand, they said among themselves, No doubt this man is a murderer, whom, though he hath escaped the sea, yet vengeance suffereth not to live. And he shook off the beast into the fire, and felt no harm.

———— *DECLARATION OF FAITH* ————

Nothing, not even the bite of a venomous snake, can hinder what God has called me to do, or thwart His Word in my life. He is above all false gods and whatever is brought against me, I will shake off into the fire and suffer no evil effects.

(Mark 16:15-20; Isaiah 55:11; Psalm 91; Luke 10:19)

PRAYER OF SALVATION

God loves you—no matter who you are, no matter what your past. God loves you so much that He gave His one and only begotten Son for you. The Bible tells us that "...whoever believes in him shall not perish but have eternal life" (John 3:16 NIV). Jesus laid down His life and rose again so that we could spend eternity with Him in heaven and experience His absolute best on earth. If you would like to receive Jesus into your life, say the following prayer out loud and mean it from your heart:

Heavenly Father, I come to You admitting that I am a sinner. Right now, I choose to turn away from sin, and I ask You to cleanse me of all unrighteousness. I believe that Your Son, Jesus, died on the cross to take away my sins. I also believe that He rose again from the dead so that I might be forgiven of my sins and made righteous through faith in Him. I call upon the name of Jesus Christ to be the Savior and Lord of my life. Jesus, I choose to follow You and ask that You fill me with the power of the Holy Spirit. I declare that right now I am a child of God. I am free from sin and full of the righteousness of God. I am saved in Jesus' name. Amen.

If you prayed this prayer to receive Jesus Christ as your Savior for the first time, please contact us on the web at **www.harrisonhouse.com** to receive a free book.

Or you may write to us at

Harrison House

P.O. Box 35035

Tulsa, Oklahoma 74153

ABOUT THE AUTHOR

James Riddle is a successful entrepreneur, educator, and Bible teacher. His unique approach to writing stirs the heart and encourages the soul. One does not have to sit under his teaching for long to know that he has a deep love for the body of Christ. It is pure joy for him to see God's children living in closeness with their Father and fulfilling the call He has on their lives.

At the center of all of James' success is his love for the Word. "In my own personal life," he says, "I have a simple mission statement. 'Be the person you are created to be.'" It is his resolute conviction that only through the Word can anyone achieve true success and be the person that God wants them to be. Therefore, the Word must always be our final authority no matter what we are facing.

It is just that attitude that caused James to write *The Complete Personalized Promise Bible.* For three-and-a-half years he researched and personalized everything the Bible says about who we are, what we have, and how we are supposed to act as Christians. It was birthed in a determination to believe the right things so he could keep his prayers in the perfect will of God. All of that research and dedication is now available to the public, and what a blessing it is!

James holds an honors degree in Creative Writing from the University of Texas at El Paso. His *Complete Personalized Promise Bible* series has sold well over 100,000 copies. He is the father of four and lovingly refers to his wife, Jinny, as his beautiful Puerto Rican princess.

James Riddle would love to hear how God has blessed you through this material. Please send your testimony to the following address:

James Riddle Ministries
P.O. Box 972624
El Paso, Texas 79997

Or email him at:
thepromisecenter@elp.rr.com

Visit James Riddle online at:
www.jamesriddle.net

ALL THE PROMISES FOR WOMEN IN AN EASY-TO-USE TOPICAL FORMAT!

Now women can find every promise in the Bible by topic in this specially designed edition. Each Scripture is personalized just like the original version and includes inspiring devotional introductions to each topic. Selected topics include:

Freedom From Fear

Encouragement

Long Life

A Successful Marriage

Children

Peace

Protection

And more!

This unique and inspiring book is perfect as a treasured gift for yourself or someone you love.

The Complete Personalized Promise Bible for Women
By James Riddle
ISBN 13: 978-1-57794-664-2

Available at fine bookstores everywhere or visit www.harrisonhouse.com.

EVERY PROMISE IN THE BIBLE IN TOPICAL FORMAT JUST FOR MEN!

This easy-to-use topical edition for men gives them all the promises specially designed for their needs. Each Scripture is personalized just like the original version and includes inspiring devotional introductions to each topic. Selected topics include:

Your Call to Leadership

Guidance

Faith

Prosperity

Knowing Your Destiny in Life

Wisdom

And more!

A powerful and life-changing gift, this unique book is perfect for yourself and others!

The Complete Personalized Promise Bible for Men

By James Riddle

ISBN 13: 978-1-57794-663-2

Available at fine bookstores everywhere
or visit www.harrisonhouse.com.

HEALING BELONGS TO YOU!

With over 100,000 of *The Complete Personalized Promise Bibles* sold, now every single promise for health and healing in the Bible is compiled in one convenient volume. Not only are these Scripture promises listed for you, but each one is accompanied by a personalized prayer and declaration of faith.

You'll discover that Jesus died to bring wholeness in every area of your life. Broken relationship and fellowship with God has now been restored. Sickness is now healed. As you review these powerful Scriptures, pray in faith, and declare the Word, the light of God's love will begin to bring healing to your life.

Recognize His love for you in its fullest measure

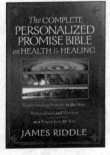 and discover that no sin, sickness, or disease will ever hold you in bondage again.

The Complete Personalized Promise Bible on Health and Healing
By James Riddle
ISBN 13: 978-1-57794-840-7

Available at fine bookstores everywhere
or visit www.harrisonhouse.com.

THE HARRISON HOUSE VISION

Proclaiming the truth and the power
Of the Gospel of Jesus Christ
With excellence;

Challenging Christians to
Live victoriously,
Grow spiritually,
Know God intimately.